I Look for Mum

Written by Susan Frame

Illustrated by Valeria Issa

Collins

I look for Mark in his room.

2

I dash into the garden.

I look near the rocket.

I can not see Mark.

Jibber barks.

Bow wow!

He barks at the chair.

Look! A coat with feet and hair!

Is it Mark?

Yes! Mark is in the coat.

Meet Mark.

Look for Mark

🐾 Review: After reading 🐾

Use your assessment from hearing the children read to choose any GPCs, words or tricky words that need additional practice.

Read 1: Decoding

- Take turns with the children to find and point to a word in which two letters make one sound, e.g. l/oo/k, r/oo/m, g/ar/d/e/n, s/ee, c/oa/t. Ask the children to sound out and read the word.
- Challenge the children to find and read the two words in which three letters stand for one sound. (page 6: *n/ear*, page 9: *ch/air*, page 10: *h/air*)

Read 2: Prosody

- Model reading each page with expression to the children. After you have read each page, ask the children to have a go at reading with expression.
- On pages 10 and 11 show children how you use a surprised tone for the exclamations and a questioning voice for the questions.

Read 3: Comprehension

- Turn to pages 14 and 15. Encourage the children to retell the story as if they were the girl, using the pictures as prompts. They could look back through the story and reread the text, too.
- For every question ask the children how they know the answer. Ask:
  - Where does the girl look for Mark first? (*in his room*)
  - Was the girl in a hurry to find Mark? How do you know? (e.g. *Yes, she dashes into the garden to find him.*)
  - Who found Mark first? How do you know? (*Jibber, because Jibber barks*)
  - Do you think Mark found a good hiding place? Why? (e.g. *Yes, because it took a while for the girl to find him./No, because his legs and hair were sticking out.*)